wide ass of night

KRISTI MAXWELL

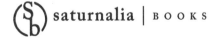 saturnalia | BOOKS

Distributed by Independent Publishers Group
Chicago

Saturnalia Books
2816 North Kent Rd.
Broomall, PA 19008
info@saturnaliabooks.com

ISBN: 978-1-947817-82-1 (print), 978-1-947817-83-8 (ebook)
Library of Congress Control Number: 2024949075

Cover art and book design by Robin Vuchnich

Distributed by:
Independent Publishing Group
814 N. Franklin St.
Chicago, IL 60610
800-888-4741

TABLE OF CONTENTS

THE RIND IS THE FRUIT'S OBITUARY, COMPOSED AHEAD OF ITS DEATH

to open communication the way of kimchi
between the gut and the brain
                              microorganisms disrupting
the individual's fiction   yet again

how often the fact becomes the metaphor

that flaunts   its veneer of sturdiness
what one might not undermind
undermine   the femur on this leg of thought
still with room to lengthen

the word seduces the letter from its alphabet
builds a landscape out of a typeface's anatomy
limiting ascenders   limiting ascendence

words tethered to domination

later we'll travel   to see sea wrack
gathered like underwire at the base of the mounds
of sand   sea wrack for the shore's rack
ha   as laughter continues to write the biography
(biographeme) of a face

              still   they had become abbreviations
of themselves

                    orange rind in an orange mug

TIME OF THE MONTH

The blister confirms your boots
are mad cows. You move.
There is pain. A different kind
than you imagined yesterday
after a longtime friend said, of writing
poetry, *maybe I'm always just trying*
to interrupt myself. As a blister interrupts
a body's bounded-ness. You sit
and wait for something to pour out.
What an earnest urn. Large enough
to cater to the event of your own life.
A cuppa. A copula, linking self to action.
Now, go—feeling it, really feeling it.

*

From the penis cometh the bouquet of blooms from a Bradford Pear. Ceramic
mischief. Your baby holds his mouth like the drawing of a mountain or volcano
(there is a flatness where should be a peak). The ocean wants your shadow, as if it's
a dark spume left over from the rushing of your body up the water-weighted sand.
Usually, you're in Michigan, but today's geo-tag says Oregon, so I can guess the
water's name. The sky looks inflamed around the whitehead sun no one will just yet
pop. How many of us have moved our living rooms to the yard, lighting floor lamps
with extension cords, self consciously picking at whatever has dried on the knee-
high table. Whose knee. You are populated by syllables, the usual suspects whom
you now line up, the criminal word locked away. The body a penitentiary. The body
its own charging station. Changing room. The body a toll, a tall order, etc. See that
shimmer there, signaling something.

*

A model train moves toward the tunnel between your legs from the origin point between his legs. A genital allegory, not even close to derailing our training, though speaking to its capacity to be derailed. You gaze to the side, away from the engine, whose steam, because a pencil drawing, looks like a condom taking on wind or a clumsy gun aiming away from your body towards his. Where would the bullet land. I have lingered too long here, perhaps, when the next infinity pool awaits, the next fraying thatched roof. Instead, a telephone booth the color of cherry blossoms, a bunny squatting beside a skeptical child. You grow cabbage better than you ever grew your confidence.

*

Maybe the poem is just the inbox's message: injured fox.

*

Fireside, someone thumb-wrestles Jesus. Jesus might win, despite, in comparison, the length and width of her thumb. Her tacked-on beard, a basket for the rest of her face. A description of pharmaceutical side effects is juxtaposed with an image in a public place, this time a dark pint on a lighter bar. Perfect stretch marks of grain. Elsewhere, a cloud that could be a blob of ricotta, soloing on a blue plate of sky. Of course, it's special. You hold your hair back. Your tiredness digs ditches on your face for the shadow's thirst to lay itself before being covered up. The cactus grows its soft megaphone. You'd like your nails to be petals, but they're not. Stay tuned for what has yet to be announced.

*

Wearing your fatigue. Soldiering on. Soldering day to day to build your own time-
table. Gathering thyme after the sage tells you to. Enough. There's no grazing in
your field of vision today. Your gaze a drought. Your dough-eyes, dried, like blood at
the deer's mouth. The bow of the *D* in need of an arrow and an aim. My own name
shoots through me. A pinball machine with jammed ramps.

*

From the horizon of your bright arms, your bright face has risen, and I venture out
on the substantial pier of your thoughts and I am already a rotting plank there on
which the birds have created a floor plan with the miniature tablecloths of their
shits, assigning who to what table, abandoning symmetry for the kinds of righteous
chaos suitable to bodies' factories, bossed by no one. You sit atop a makeshift bench
of bags of beech smoked barley malt. The noticeable give suggests the bags will
hold you even after you get up. You are given the choice between *almost* and *despite*.
Like a city planner, grammar determines the sentence's skyline. You hold the tallest
building in your mouth. A replicate tongue.

*

Upon observing the lemon bejeweled with mold, you ask to no one, Who even
noticed the earth's grillz when it first smiled on us?

*

You hear the water registering the shape of his body, then you hear it stop. He's standing now in the doorway, soap making a well-whittled arrowhead of his hair. The shower takes him back, like you would, were he ever to leave. Pain revises our lives. You roll the mat out then unfold the tent of your body to set up on its field. Let go of the question about how your best compares to a flower's best. Let go of specific flowers, each with its own list of strengths, including what it requires of the sun. One is praised for how little one needs.

*

The hellos have ended. You have not taken yourself outside. You push a cat you love away because her silver hair interferes with your dress. What has happened to all the roller brushes that quiet the need to evaluate the effects of each intimacy. Because of proliferate dead skin cells, we are often in one another's mouths. What tools we have for taking away. The cat lays out. Her matted fur makes her look like she's covered in Venetian blinds someone has partially opened. The light from the window reminds you to look.

*

The list of intellectual traits you might possess includes humility. The third person to love your message motivates a fourth and a fifth. Alerted again about the death of a rich man you've only heard of because of his crimes. One must decide at which point the trashcan truly cannot hold anymore. The woman who pulled out in front of you at a stop sign buys your dirty chai at the coffee shop drive-thru but not your cherry almond scone. If there's an active shooter, the first thing to do is STOP CLASS, all caps. An etcetera we move inside. A hummingbird sleeping in the hammock the flower's petal becomes. One suspects there's somewhere right now one animal devouring another animal. Animals inside others. Elsewhere, the rain is giving eyes to a pavilion, pooling into eye-shaped pools.

*

You mouth the nipple of an amateur macaron. The human wherever it is willed.

*

The platform shakes. The body, too. We drink a Green Line at the Blue Line off the Blue Line. 'I' drink. That long straw through which my self is sucked up from the glass of utterance, barely filled. The salve is to 'solve' / to think a thing 'solvable' / or why procedural dramas have a larger audience than poetry.

*

Sitting in piss on public transport. A mom says guess what you guys, the dinosaurs had mothers. What was a poet among them. Likely the fern—that maximalist.

*

An April snow, like the antithesis of transcendence, grounding itself, supplying a cold ink for the road to write a new story of arrival. In which the idea of melt in-builds an appreciation of the ephemeral, the dying living animal. The rival snow beats out the weaker green arms, holding up their little fists of would-be flowers, fighting chance.

*

Ricocheting between *verdict* and *Verdita Slushies, Back on the Menu*. Order in the (food) court. At the side bar. Lawdy, lawdy—and, yes, fingers crossed, I am "turnin' 40," as if it were a head trapped in the marvelous trap of my sauntering body in its line of sight. And perhaps this time the gaze is a gauze, fixing my own vision. Self-sense. Ascending rather than sentencing. To age in this Age of what? No more *this is all / there is / for you / from here /on out*. Hear me out, then. Hear, hear. Let's all rise.

*

In his dream of her dream, you are exactly how you are. A caption that doesn't describe a picture. Beads of Luna Night Oil make a cracked geode of your hands, which your pores take on, like a network of museums, looking to flesh out the gem and mineral rooms they have too little precious to fill. What if the artifact itself is the vitrine's mind, even if it started out as bone. We shift the posture of skeletons. Authenticity's decimal point. We press against the back of our understanding, crowded by uncertainty. Our breast must go somewhere. Decide what to face.

*

Too often confusing dinosaurs and dragons and also lamenting eggs and seeing now certain letters nesting their own eggs like the descender under the round bottom of *g*. Was it worth crying over the baby turtles the surviving contestants were told to eat. Your tear a wobbly egg birthing the glow of your face. It should be incubating. The egg doesn't birth itself. It doesn't appear to do much. This is a good enough lesson on what is meant by *pretty on the inside*. You think of that movie you repeated throughout childhood in which a man enclosed in a ship with a bulging window at its front rides through the body of a woman for whom he welcomes being made small. You imagine a tiny man going to work inside you. Preserving your molting spine. Hammering in your disc. That poorly hidden Easter egg. Pain a lawn you're made to tend. It sometimes seems the moon is a rejected egg. Nothing will squat down to warm it. You would take that job. Wide ass of night.

*

A mountain of wallpaper, by which I mean a wallpaper with a mountain design, by which I mean a wallpaper with a series of triangles with smaller triangles un-patterned within them, signifying rugged rock faces or a hard eyebrow that might double as a climber's hold, leftover—*next* and *another*, their own types of faith, implying a continuation, a movement forward, out of. I see why you miss it. As I do the little beak of iris just before it barfs out its bloom.

Maybe you aren't shitty, and the world is

Bird with cantaloupe   a second beak

The/a roof alive with squirrel sex

       Sometimes I make a caboose of his name

though I do not "take" it

as in a card in Go Fish

as in abuse

someone justifies

To suck   it up

or in general

to

       —costuming a ballerina

in part   *tu*   you

obscuring oneself with another's language

              thoughts

     For the sake of forsaking

Go away, squirrel, get on now, git

I'm not up for another description

of the way you seemed to turn

and acknowledge the gnawing

you'd done on the house

before the gun sends a bb into your body

       not a bb   he corrects me

       a pellet

poor bb   *Writhing*   an action that might be applied

to all of us

           Pain a pane that breaks

    while all we cannot house

        finds new ways in and out

        makes shift

            makes shit

            of us

            from us

    makes sit what one might otherwise stand for

They

(1)

But is the rectangle flat if it can be opened?
They question the ways they perceive the world,

the language they use: persimmon, audacious,
ruined. The day either a habit or habitable.

Among their preferred materials: wood. The kind
the tree keeps for itself. Tree, the wood's essence,

or wood, the tree's. What of branch, what of branching
out? They were asked to form their bodies into such.

A song accompanies a motion. Under a pavement,
a world still teems. The branch is a perch

for the clawed feet of the mind. They claw out of their
minds. Of course, it is painful—or so one assumes. One

assumes a position unlike a branch. One rejects shape
because the others so depend on it. They see that *share*

is chiseled out of *shape* and hold tight to the letter
that opens this. The envelope articulation is. Now slit.

To the love of sharing. To the love of their share, especially. One
is given hers. One is given over. To be for *given*, to be against.

(2)

When they anticipated their time together, they anticipated
a depth of conversation and sardines, they anticipated waterside
seating and rooftop seating, a question of masks and tastings,
ports in port cities, disinfectant small enough to pocket and
to choose whether to cart home and refill or discard,

pretending its resultant microplastics-existence will be
more micro because of its size. They anticipated they
would contribute to good and bad and less-good and less-bad
things. They questioned the verb they used to describe the savory
practice of scalping cheese, the necessity of good knifework,

one of them by far the strongest mincer. They anticipated which
would be the ones to go off to talk to fishermen and which the ones
to take too many photographs of tile, what proofs would be needed
of what actions, how their arms might come into play. They anti-
cipated skin slickening and face slackening, a wind packing heat.

They anticipated tears coaxed out by drinking and from missing
and the question of whether stars could be counted on to justify
an amount of money spent on a meal. They questioned whether
stars could be counted on more broadly, more celestially, more
astrologically. They anticipated consulting first the crab. O, Crab.

(3)

the music would not sit in them
they were bad arenas   but is the action
we want from music   *to sit*
the rump they imagine quite courageous
leaving sketches of itself   on various woods
like a lip-sticked mouth   on other surfaces
a lip sticking its landing
                    to be without music was not
to be without joy   to be without enjoinment
besides   they were not
without it   just outside it
an epidermis   the first thing that would be
punctured   they were their own
arrival gates   waiting for themselves
to show up   but it was like them
to call everything   themselves
after first contact   after the first wave
          (see they learned something from the sound
of music if not the feel of it   impalpable penetration)
                                   having committed
to the thought   that
poetry is a language that squirms

                                   they sought out
the earworm   the ancient animal
that knew a thing or two   about lodging
about

                                   how to remain

On Being Off

I was nothing but a tear-inducing blue, a water tailored by wind, pinned and loosened, made to fit your memory of my country, made to cover the whole of it. I was the blended beans and the cheekbone of oil you gave your own mouth in this portrait of consumption. Like the placard on the house overlooking a caldera, you are welcome to secret dreams. You are welcome to secrete dreams, like a musk, in hopes of attracting me, forgetting it's you who will have to move. You can make me many things in your mind, in your sketches, in the anecdotes where you'll boast I was yours, but I'll remain immovable. I'll remain unmoved. I do regret you decided not to let me stain your white swimsuit in my acrid spring and that you didn't test what I could do to your silver ring, but we won't pretend I asked for anything, disinterested as I am in your discourse, in the attribution of action to a god. I could have made ruins of you, but I didn't want your body visited like that.

Scroll

Age resembles inflection   what we stress   uplift, let fall

A human you love is the same age as a human I love

Palo santo burning at one's chest

smoke reaching up like hair in underwater portraits

you wonder the price of

and how one holds one's face in a flattering way

air-puffed   or the methods one learns to deny the self's inflation

A seafoam guitar cannot fool the desert

though your music is a kind of wetness

        a train track covered in confetti

A cast does to the arm what the tide does to the shore

but the earth will not recover

We continue to eat

We peer into the pizza's cave

where its hibernation is its journey toward its final cave

the sewer by way of the human mouth

or does the pizza cease upon digestion

and so is never sewer-bound

We undo

A selfie in the dark with no flash

A magnifying glass in a room in which everything is oversized

Scabiosa   a porous welt swelling atop a stem

        a flower bled by a butterfly   glorious leech

A human you love is in the same font as a human I love

It's hard to determine what the thread is becoming

but maybe a baguette

A gold most bread-like

*

"a smile is like a blush—it is a response, not an expression per se"

Glancing, the partial body behind her head

the legs   from knee to foot

of someone lying down

appear to be a braid

lengthening her own short hair

The clouds are clearly words furiously erased

with a film of eraser dust no one has bothered

to brush away

*

A new turtle paddles through the moon

a fool's moon   like every other

stamped on sea-lacquered sand

You go on

repositioning the gaze as a site

of transformative justice

Your street's been dead this year

A neighbor widowed two months after his wedding

A mother   clamoring off her porch with Narcan

It's fine that you need to hover over the newly unhatched

like a moon   To cheer it on

a metonym for your questionable hope

Controlled by the Great Blah-blah

it's possible you're a subtitle

with an error based on mishearing

or on failing   to comprehend

It's possible you've been turned off   all together

altogether

*

The park is a backdrop for a slice of orange

A sand dollar a shield guarding an envelope's address

A lighthouse's arranged light tutors a bride's train

I, too, would be proud of my loaf

if it were your loaf

I, too, would think the nearby water

a sufficient reason to toast

*

The sky confirms the rock formation's thigh gap

[ominous music]

[melancholy music]

[brackets hold the bodies of words like tables in morgues—

platforms for scrutinizing] [pulled out from the cold wall of the page]

Slide on in

A window gives its lecture of light to a tiled floor

which the floor only partially absorbs

"In the next slide…"

Her in her yellow dress   moving like a new expression

the public square hadn't yet learned

though its palm tree had, nodding in the breeze

*

Among decorative crumbs

your lips match your tinted lenses

A collage in which god

uses a ViewFinder

and trademarks an outstretched hand

The backpack creates a new animal

out of your walking

In this one, a psychedelic crab

and be-hatted skeleton wait

for an elevated train

and the sun is a morsel that tempts

an ineffectual pincer

A water's surface is grey like certain cooked meats

Someone is hungry

The ocean's ebb is an aging app

creping the water's skin

It is good to be reminded that sometimes

a herd of hippos is what's visible

through binoculars

How to position oneself

amidst those with knowledge

of a couch's identity   its proper name

Chesterfield or davenport (little *d* like a sideview

of the couch itself, pushed up against the wall of one's teeth)

Sometimes we call a cage a crate

and turn it into a lesson in power

romanticized by the term "to tame"

which sounds like a basic love

Elementary French

A learner who takes on the name Snow

whitening the field of herself

Another Monique

Elsewhere one patterns her ravioli

off of starfish   some impasta

unable to grow itself back

The self a greenhouse

with the sprouts on different schedules

so sometimes there is lushness

and at others   not so much

One must trust what the dirt

might still have left to tell

—its musty authority

We ask again who has it

We call again for the dirt

though we should have called to it

outside idiom   outside for real

*

In the face of climate change

on the face of the earth

at face value

value effaced

every trip feels like a farewell tour

goodbye, water inside the caldera

goodbye, sulphurous spring

*

And if the body is nothing more than bone's echo, holler, bone

But we know an echo is not an answer

even if an affirmation

How might you interpret a desire to attend to each other like drones

to attend to each other without context

without war or landscape

Could it be done?

The body is yes on the verge

of yesterday

A rosebush revived

In the aerial view of the wave pool, humans are sprinkles lodged in the icing the water becomes in its breaking

Broken water, broken thirst

That *slake* contains a body of water from which we would be advised not to drink

That a body can soothe in only certain ways

Among the places one would not like to be

even there one would like to *be*, to not be loosened from her verb

unless liking being is hard for her, is hard for him, is hard for them

A collection of crude embroideries alongside a masterful dinosaur

Enough with extinctions

*

A word is exorcised from a word.

It is yours to say now.

You come into a month as if into an inheritance,

which I guess it is. Another day, another group text

about an excess of blood. Doctor, doctor. Iron,

rest. A finger-made heart that will soon give way to a fickle heat.

(The heart was made of body *and* breath.)

I fill out a review on my app just for the enthusiastic "good job!"

it generates. What do you need to hear?

*

Not seeing is a flower

or a translation.

Fingers positioned so as to be legs

with one pant leg on

or maybe a thigh-high.

Anything to explain what's missing.

It's as if hair were coming off of her

like steam. Such a beverage.

Tall drink, etc. An ancient watermelon

inside of which are spirals of meat

and seed. I don't want to bring

the space-word in. As if it were a stray.

The live-stream at the cat café tells me

today's guests are named after cereal and pizza

—I mean, couldn't you just "eat them up?"—

before saying, no, nevermind,

these are not named after pizza at all.

Here's Weston, Easton, Florence. Here's Frances.

*

A new turtle braces itself

having learned from

its first encounter

with a wave

ocean ocean oh shit

Hey

The ocean braces itself

lays braces

across the teeth

of the shore

Yet nothing gets straightened out

The root, you ask, the root?

You misheard *taught*

when she said *tautology*

Nothing was learned

despite our circling around it

Girdles of the earth

*

Snow is its own elegy   composed of melt

a sled leaves its sheet music behind

that tracks

Why is it the breast feels like an ornament

on the tall tree of you

To choose take

it off   or take offence

                              a wind-whipped cheek

to be a Greta welcomed on a pier

to be a net in a catamaran   pleasantly weighted down

          The little prince could write

with the drawing of a quill

                    but not us—

                    not us

*

To eat Elvis, draw Elvis
on a cookie, then bite

To eat eyeless
men? A cartoonish submarine into which

no one may fit?

The image is all
that needs

changing

Slathered in streetlight

your painted cheek is pretty as snow

The outline you give your eye, as if it were
to draft itself

An essay on seeing

The manmade lens

The whole human in fact "manmade"
inside the bright lab of another body

Unfollow the turtle onto whom has been soldered wheels

There is a carrot yet to be peeled
A carrot yet to rot

despite a name's smuggling

Care-rot

A speed bump inside oneself

Get over it

To specify "goldenrod" or "canary"
To un-narrate a story   turning "I" into a slit
other words will sew up

Healing was bound to come
its little possum nose sowing night into the field
the moon disrobed

just earlier

while I sat looking for the poem

*

It was a very American narrative

To Be Sometimes Quite Resourceful

balm made from what had been gathered

the sun used

weeks' old blueberries somehow still edible

another "is" argument

another is not

on the hunt for the tagger of a friend's

art

as one tags another friend

in a photo in which they do not appear

the poem's first book

replaced with a sea

how "somehow" renders cause elusive

how language is used

to support not knowing

the corrosive water

eating through the shell of a crab

the shells of crabs

the toast going cold

*

I want to bring out the red scissors and cut two-piece scissors out

of red construction paper and add paper fasteners so the paper scissors

can be made

to perform

the action of cutting.

I want to steal pubic hair from each of my friends

to adhere to a canvas to compose a merkin flag

to raise on Independence Day as a reminder our country

is made from exploited bodies.

Yes, I will have exploited my friends.

I will be culpable.

I will be responsible.

I will be irresponsible.

I misremember.

"Misremember," a redundancy, as memory's genre is fiction, is "creative"

nonfiction, which is a way of lodging saying

in experience.

Fort Experience, Camp Experience. Come, little campers, come.

To misremember then is to remember.

I watched the other day

a video of a woman with long red nails

painting the curl of a potato peel red and attaching it to a pencil sharpener

which she then inserted her finger into

so it looked as if she had mutilated her finger—

such a small costume.

I wonder how many would overlook it

and if that would make her sad or frustrated, ready to make

pronouncements about the quality of human attention in the 21st century.

I myself am still sad, as I've been for many years,

that we haven't figured out a way to apply a knowledge of taxidermy

to a dream.

I've invented sounds I'm unwilling to give to anything

but the dream's mounted body and am afraid now they will be lost.

I imagine a beak. A red beak. Of course I would go bird

with my imagining. The dream always seems to hover above us

like a thought bubble or a crude drawing of a very fat or puffy sheep.

*

"Find you one who can do both"

As "freaked" can with Schuyler and Milton

Sky-lure   Moon-bait   That comet could be

a cosmic tadpole   Surely we can find a frog

in a campus of stars   An artificial lake

Check the time again   Ten 'til

5-0, 5-0   the ninth hour being tailed then put away

It's okay if we have to find ways to like engaging with the world

The cross-sections of sandwiches

The quesadilla's overstuffed seam

Today I wonder if I'm much more than a name leaving someone's mouth

A palm frond pinned against night

Specimen

Spacemen

O, naughty astronaut   sneaking tortilla chips

Like the sensitive poet, friable

It seems innocent until the puncture

Ways to avoid the viral droplet

or to break the delicate envelope

a robe on the microbe

Its fragility a boon to our own

I snubbed an old friend in a dream, guest-bartending, doing badly

out of clean glasses, unable to intervene when the register stuck out

its long tongue of receipts

He was reading Beckett's *Molloy*

and not among those I asked to jump

when I asked everyone to jump

in unison

*

Babies are still happening

A rhino in North Carolina

An okapi just up the road

And living walls in living rooms

       in offices   purification decoration

             (ration) (ration) (don't hoard)

Somewhere a tart is oozing

Sweet wound

With plastic and duct tape, a makeshift barricade

allows an old man, driving for an app, to continue

driving, amidst a novel anxiety

The galaxy is just one of the many options

available to have reproduced

on the swimsuit

What we will take to the waters

What we will take down with us

But think of it

to float in one's own galaxy

one that came at such an agreeable cost

one we could "live with"

*

We were fooled by the images of dolphins
in place of gondolas in bright canals. We had hope

all we had done could be easily undone.

We had
feared all
we had done

no one would recall.

We would be
a clear water no body could get to. We would be
unaccessed.

Ready to support life, but

isolated—unable to convey

this preparedness, this willingness, this open room.

*

You with your foam-made leaf

You with your cloud-buttered hillside

You with your hand hovering

reiki-like over a llama

What hurts?

Your hand is a cupboard for miniature toy weapons

The usual

candlestick, revolver, knife

a special edition poison

Our palms look cut open and healed

We are someone's memory

another person's prediction

A woman in a long fuchsia skirt

with a tall fuchsia drink

who may in fact be the drink's projection

Each self   a screen

*

Here are some letters arranged into a spell.

A violent triangle shape

Arrow's head

Eros's mapping

on which we chart our own longings.

Today, I want simply

for my husband to get home

and the singularity

of that desire embarrasses me.

I know there is more to want.

*

Changed "raining this bad" to "raining this much"

and set a reminder in my phone

to draw you a bath

on a sheet of paper

to make you laugh

*

The Bibb lettuce has finally gone in

like someone brave

fortified by friends

proclaiming she will do it

she will do it

She's going in

But really the Bibb lettuce is not

like that at all

It just lay there

getting covered by dirt

no blanket

Most I suspect

would have little idea

as to what they are to become

What a life!—to join

with bigger bodies, to be

taken in, digested—

a whole part

A logic that can hold

numerous slaughters

—an argument of priority

deploying the "common" word

We will make sense

when we must

We will make sense

like a garment or bread

when we need it

*

Can you burn a burn

erase what has been   erased

re-delete un-un-

The urn was your own body

How well you held the ash

A cigarette smoldering and upright

So much untapped

Whole wells unused

Say *drought* again

Emphasize the hurt inside

ow ow ow

We were so close

We neared each other

We missed

To illustrate the phrase *pick up your butts*

you drew hands cupping a human backside

I drew a littered ground, slashed through

Still   we got there

guided by differences

not deterred by them

*

slug of aloe   of

we have forgotten nearly   of

there are other ways to die

of this   of this   of this

we look to the concrete

slug   slug   slug   slug

to be where we are

*

The endless stream ends

"You're All Caught Up"

perhaps in the fishing line of images

Someone sees your sunset

and raises you a moon

Another fence has been given a face

You've been using your hand

to measure portions of protein

From the palm to first knuckle

Rubber bullet sized   you now know

The body feels to be yours

Feel again

*

Beside a friend searching

for images of genital warts

some of which recall hens-of-the-wood

and why not? Fungal messages—the body

interrupts with its knowledges

including the brain's suspicion

a wart is not a fungus

though a knot in flesh

(now the tree again, whose own labial

bark is suffused with knots

alongside its clinging mushrooms—

fine enough shelves—see how the water

sits there—edible shelves that teach

the trees to fear less their own shelf-futures)

Timber! Tremor! Tumor! (Another monstrous

growth) That we give the verb "grow"

to the tumors. A vegetable verb. A flower.

A tumor *gnaws*. Can language want

to treat it like a carnivore? No, I doubt

it's language that *wants*. The body has decided

as it's wont to do

its own language

though we may not discover it

ever or in time or inside time—

that crate in which we're made obedient

*

Reminiscing about the beanbags of Lithuania

about a jeweler finding a boat in the amber

mounting it then upon a copper fragment

it's easy enough to imagine

a piece of a lake

set atop the lake of our own body

always already a body a water

We are composed that way

Less song-like than dredged up

Our death never not with us

even before it says hi, waving its tidal wave

*

"Sell your ideas/ they are totally acceptable"

Regurgitative poetics   taking up as a fly takes

The fly tattooed on your wrist

a reminder of the constancy of your own decay

The stench of your food-self wafting

You   waffle

The sail that looks like a citrus slice,

high-fived by the sun

She would rather sea herself than see herself

I'll say no more

ALPINE INTERLUDE

double-edged abecedarians

(1)

About having been birthed a crab:
body a holding tank for tears. As on Mont Blanc,
coldness muzzles the avalanche. Here, only oneself is buried.
Dredge or don't. Like elephants prone
either to favor the right or left tusk, the face a shelf
filled with chipped things. The fig
given by the tree is not metaphorical, accompanied by a sigh,
hot in summer's throat, with gratitude to the wasp that deposits its I—
immature fruit enticing the insect inside, questionable swaraj.
Jus? The goo existence resorts to. A hack
knifes through a seemingly impregnable system. All
lost as leather an awl eats. That to make can mean to maim.
Monitoring the beloved's Fitbit dashboard again,
notice the impenetrability of the dream state, the border so
obstinately tended, a mouth guard protecting the teeth of sleep—
preponderance of consciousness. What a tranq
quiets reanimates, upright as a needle upright. And after,
roses abandon, if not their vibrational frequencies, their hurts.
Slow motion is said to be the speed of tragedy, but
tonight, fast-forward oversees this smothering adieu
under which your lips form a shape one can't improv.
Visited by a shield-backed Picasso bug we first saw
where it wasn't to be seen, we pondered nature's tax,
xanthic attempts to terrestrialize the sun, a way to pay.
Youth unwraps its own box, fondles the fuzz.
Zero in now—sing, having hawked up your aria.

(2)

awoken by avalanche cannons, making sob
cling-less snow down the mountain's face, unelated
even though sun-pinked hours earlier, as if
gratified, tickled by light's soft cough,
its idiom for the dark swoon the horizon—that DJ—
knowingly promotes, we tug lucidity's skin, desire to heal,
milking the bed for a final ounce of sleep, worn
out, worn down like a cheap sole, clop-
quenched; since now the temperature is no fever,
since never again the minute will be mistook for vast,
unlike the valley's id or the toothbrush turned shiv,
weaponized, as the mind can be, we vex
yesterday, failing any longer to water its schmaltz

Bury

That the four crabs were dead already

when the girl gathered them

when the girl named them

Tinker, Tailor, Soldier, and Sailor

evoking choice as fundamental

when the girl asked them if they wanted

to live under her bed

when the girl gave them an answer

and the mother noticed a smell

and the mother evicted

Death gets to decide

the girl learned

though in truth she couldn't have kept them

either way

she shouldn't have kept them

The lip of shore wore them like piercings

The girl idolized the sea

A perfect little fan

A shell-mimic

Made of herself an autograph book

Gave the full page of her body

for that signature

At least then she would always have

the sea of herself to touch

to love

How to find that page

How to find that book

The body's library large

and largely unstewarded

The wrong things catalogued

On Failure

I taught a book with a rape in it

I taught a book that referenced a rape

in its penultimate chapter

The disclosure made a student

feel betrayed   her protagonist

this protagonist   this narrator

she had been listening to

this rapist narrator not narrating

the rape   but being told about it

decades later by the one he had

raped   a park scene

maybe   a strangely shaped kite

I taught a book with a rape in it

and did not condemn the rapist

or the author who decided for his narrator

to rape   I asked questions about

discourses of consent   I betrayed

my student with these questions

Rape apologist she said

not to me   Rape apologist she said

to the Dean of Students   Did I teach

a book with a rape in it   I taught

a book   nothing   I taught a student

nothing   I taught a book with a rape

in it   with bed bugs   with medical

school   with a street forced to meet

an inevitable rain   I "taught" a book

there was betrayal   there were betrayals

there was a rape   there were rapes

there are many rapes   many many

The book did not change that   the book

did nothing   the book changed me

in relation to the student   I see the "dent"

there now   the damage awaiting the wreck

STROLL
pedestrian sonnets

*

A fire hydrant has been made to wear a purple loofah like a fascinator, as if waiting for a plume of water to spurt.

The obstinate beak of an arrow does not open, but speaks nonetheless.

A dandelion, then a yellow door.

Someone has set a reflector inside the belly of a plastic rabbit—our eyes maybe safe enough warrens for the little light it births.

I want that that net be open.

"Public Art": a jewel-tone horse no one is permitted to ride, a suitcase discarded at a driveway's edge, both at home and not.

A green lace failing to learn from grass, sitting atop it like an aristocrat, waiting for the stalled litter to be lifted, though the blades are coming instead.

But then the tenderness of a gnarled tree hugging a weathered timber post—to hear "tomb me" when the beloved pleads, "come back to me."

The Mary statuette looks like a low-rent ghost from behind, sheet excessively starched, hangers unbent, rebent, their soul singular and in the closet, a bone no X-ray could find.

A lawn replaced with a pollinating garden.

Like the Outhere Brothers, like Peter Gabriel, like ourselves along with the radio, the buds of the knockout roses sing *boom, boom, boom*, and why not?— explosions loom.

No cicada shells, but a friend asking who will come over for cicada paella, showing a recipe he has found.

What is peripheral to a wellness center.

Just like it for something to emerge and become a resource rather than a wonder.

*

The recipe's parenthetical (farro like sorrow).

Mistook a wet chia seed for a tick.

To be a gorilla making little food songs.

The barbershop had been a barbershop and was a sneaker shop in between.

No lengthy engagement with color, but remembering learning the barber's red and white pole signaled the performing of bloody services—a used rag unloosing itself in some milky solution, an elegant abject scarf.

A pimple you won't stop fingering, a bulb alerting you to an onion's distress.

Twin tigers or a tiger and a mirror?

And if we are just trees of blood covered over with a mitten of flesh needing darning, gosh darn.

More masks than partial Styrofoam cups—this season's urban tumbleweed.

A vine loops and unfurls like an illustration of sperm or like model cursive, but just a sequence of letters and not a word, just a knot, securing something, even in its illegibility.

Our dead skin multiplies us, (un)makes us in two-plus places at once.

Chain link, chain link, fenceless—kick ball change.

A tentacle of people outside the ice cream shop, another tentacle loosely attached to an open house.

The florist replaced with a doctor—re-placed; the volta's inbuilt.

*

The fossil sings, *fa sol la ti*, at the Falls of the Ohio—a desire for ourselves to find ourselves.

Two bike locks but neither key.

An incline doing less now to one's thighs.

The cottonwood seeds, accumulating again, like summer snow in the path's margins.

A lime green wallet on a lime green railing by a drink with a lime scissoring its rim—you'll think "sexual," then question, "sexual?"

Is an assword a type of safe word, someone asks, seeing the "p" erased from the password on the chalkboard.

The basket of sweet breads photographs well but each—and you try a bite from each—tastes stale.

The frequency with which "impossible" is inaccurate.

To call it "Of an Age" or to call it "Short-lived."

To relish the slow poke.

The science the science the science the yellow brick road.

Hard to catch the light going out— noticing later that it has.

We find ourselves repeating "the numbers."

The slimming diet an eraser is intent on, despite the fashion, itself another snow.

*

How a cut makes it seem blood's so anxious to get out.

Reading the word "curiously" at the moment "curing" pops up—occurs?—in a reminder (*Check curing garlic—may need another week*).

To have reservations—but where or about what/whom?

The fountain with its slim fingers of water that make it look like it's scratching the sky's welts.

A tree with sudsy clusters gathered on the glassy skin of its leaves.

A few houses side by side with stones arranged like turkeys or someone holding and fanning out terrific or terrible swords of light.

Where the painted crayon looks like a condiment bottle more so than a crayon, "We build our kids for the future" rather than a future for "our kids."

He knows the yucca, I know the poppy.

Dairy Del, it turns out, short for Dairy Delicious—we walk through the drive-thru when the walk-up window is closed.

Duct tape encircling the bicep of the tree one learns is a gypsy moth caterpillar barrier, an insect a misguided artist made into a pest, carting it home like a new pigment.

Eight rolled rugs set out for junk day, pattern-in, but we don't stop, so we don't see the patterns.

A house the color blue water never is, a flower the color of a house.

To call the new cardinal a "little dude" doesn't seem fitting, but neither does your hand as a provisional nest, so you just go with it.

Here, the porch stairs are designed to be welcoming, widening toward the road, giving the impression of opened arms.

*

The thing that had changed was your decisions.

Paramour or paronomasia?—that both speak to a doubling, to a disruption of an illusion of containment, i.e., the pun is a punk, inherently, in its rejection of stability, in its brazen infidelity, a marveling in displacement—and the human aspires.

An account of psychic geographies.

Eyes best described as "bulbous" or as blood blisters.

The ubiquity of a rice grain, that it can operate as a unit of measurement: "Ideally, the hairs will be the length of a rice grain" in order for the wax to attach.

Pumping stations at Reservoir Park don't help with dismantling the Earth Mother metaphor.

That's a long green, unlike a long face—an efficient car stops & starts & startles.

An eventless countdown.

Toothy shadows, biting at an abstraction in the concrete.

A reminder that cities become rather than are.

What is the tensest tense?

You compromise on a mile, and he speaks the last quarter in German you forget, again, he knows.

It would've been alright to live, he says, before trailing off—a cicada shell he lobbed still clinging to your dress.

O dark brooch.

*

Didn't mean a soul's friction, though that's what you heard, my sandal at odds with the day's humidity.

Among those who've learned the mushroom's favored habitat.

The bush makes a sound, its animal-organ shifting—another tumorous body dealing with its occupation.

More wreckage at the intersection with a streetlight than at the intersections without.

Replace what do you care with how do you care.

A flower that looks like a gramophone showroom—not a little galaxy, but a bottle-sturdy hurtsickle, said to hurt the sickle that tries to take it down; bachelor's button; cornflower; blue blob; gogglebuster—a bouquet of names I'm happy to carry in my mouth, to transplant into the soiled mind, whatever good that might do, trusting it might do some good.

Of course it was the one place you didn't warn to watch your step that your mother fell.

The single mother waxing you waxing on about mothering and her preference for descriptive words rather than judgment words when talking with her little girl and your own awkward evaluation: *sounds like you're doing a good job*.

The cat on the porch ready to go in.

The point of this was not to scrutinize the boundary between inside and outside or even the idea of boundary, bounded-ness, etc.

Already dispersed.

A prayer list's sanctioned gossip.

Timber—timbre; wood-tone—would tone?

An imaginary friend who just ups and moves on—a goodbye letter hypothesized
to have been maybe written in invisible ink you just didn't know and would never
learn how to activate.

*

It's raining so you look up virtual walks on YouTube and end up in a rainforest in Hawaii, near the place an aunt and uncle were born.

The sun keeps jutting in as if it's prohibiting the view, a slash through it—or a seatbelt, perhaps, securing it during this collision.

Bird sounds draw the camera up.

You consider muting and Norway 4K – Scenic Relaxation with Calming Music, but worry over the relationship between making mute and making extinct, not wanting to contribute any more to that kind of project.

Someone in the comments wants for only a little herb, and another talks to god.

There's a bird that sounds like packing tape being ripped off a cardboard box.

Something has arrived.

You hover over Canada and turn the location services off in each app on your phone.

A desire path is your favorite way of moving from point to point because it reminds you of a poem's unsanctioned routes.

But language is always the long way and never the short cut.

Don't @ me—a cork done in by a corkscrew, if one were to lean over to look @ that inedible danish.

Don't *but acronyms.*

The scenic is disrupted by a commercial, by the commercial.

Is that a road or water whose sound now seeps in?

*

Two points below exceptional—a credit sore.

To be a mutation once considered un-druggable.

He shows me a video where aid looks a lot like violence.

The rejection of quotation marks as the refusal of further enclosure—a thought while thinking about C.D. Wright's *One Big Self* and seeing plantlife's exercise in mobility, sometimes thwarted.

You never had understood what was meant by a color cruise, but liked what you imagined better than what you learned.

They run off the field, you walk to the kitchen, after first a walk to the bathroom.

Another new set of rules, another nest rejecting the concept of Nature.

A dry first half, a wet second—as if time itself were sopping.

And aren't we drenched by it?

Walk back on.

A fruit bowl overflowing with sour ovaries.

In the blue, with the rain stopped, a referee seeming to control the rain—sun a yellow card, a warning.

Whistle on.

All just slightly off.

*

The biplane looks like an unhesitant *h* or squat *I*, adamant its presence be known. The swimming hole doesn't require the swimmer; orient yourself by the bridge.

Among the walks you've pieced together from reading, Dostoevsky's white-night-dependent madness of missing darkness, superior.

The long chew of Portobello jerky.

The king chew for which your teeth are the servile countryside.

No need to fear silliness, space maker.

May may warm back up.

Mei-mei, little sister, the name of the older cat.

The periplus—it came to me, now carrying within it the husband's name, like good goods, but we won't talk of trading.

You end up in a cul de sac and think of a uterus; turn back.

I agree it is worth challenging the myth of who wants it more gets it.

We don't deserve and aren't served by it, despite its little tray of serving, folded out.

To be flexible as an unclear referent.

Seems to be clearing up.

*

Deafening.

The death of someone whose size never exceeded a stocking.

The porch is a late night—so know what you're committing to.

Hate yourself less.

There's someone who doesn't at all.

The cat grooming sounds like a precious knock on a miniature door, the size for a dollhouse.

Sometimes you take a tongue to your skin—typically, to meet blood.

You go over responses to the never-guest's family emergency.

The girl says if you find a boy, he will stop making noise when you hold him.

Conch dreams.

The water 78 degrees.

Count it out.

He holds the hot dog in a provocative, if juvenile way.

You're still dripping.

*

Snow what?

Do you *Like Water for Chocolate* or *Water for Elephants*?—pseudo-cento—a question again of (re)sources.

Saying at the same time, *there it is.*

One never truly changes her mind, never wipes the baby bottom of that bad thought, never locates the spare to replace what tires her.

As if a ship that must make it through the worst mood of the sea.

I could go on.

There is a basement to clean, a hustle to have.

This one's trying to climb.

Who's documenting?

A friend who catalogues encounters with abandoned toothpicks—what detached tusks might look like, amateurly drawn.

A mind stops bossing a mouth.

When "Benny and the Jets" comes on you try to think of a dog you just recently met rather than about backyard karaoke with the friend who's moving—perhaps if you liked dogs more you could stay still in that image, but instead you squirm, and, like you imagine would do an unruly baby, you fall to the floor where it seems okay to cry, where it seems perhaps even expected.

It pretends well for our future.

Sleep uses a pillow to write its thesis on the materiality of dreams onto a cheek—too superficial to last, but still you check it out.

*

Other things happen in the face of loss—upon the collagen-firm jawline of loss, on the slick forehead, within the clenched fists of pores.

Then that awful bit for me to ha-ha about.

My judgy drunk-self says I just don't care anymore, while I'm crying.

If you hold your body a certain way, like a fibrous page to light.

The fandom around abuse.

It became too much.

I didn't do enough of anything.

Was it disgust you had or a question about those neon pink and purple flowers in a neighbor's window box, deforming your own love of artifice.

A bird-parent carts back two worms and a cicada the three trips you notice—what you had mistook for weeks for human whistling was avian, and you felt better about the neighbor.

You'll never get over the slug conducting the orchestral slime of itself with its own elegant batons.

All of those half-attempts at an external music, while the sound worked inside.

To go on playing an iris in the beanbag's lens—to inflate the papasan in four breaths.

Dividing the length value by 1760, one discovers 2000 yards in miles.

The length value—the value of the length of this gaffe.

*

It wasn't a dream, it was a flood – Frank Stanford

A little joke I make for myself: writing a *Perryiod* piece for my Perry, but set when?

Not sure EATUUP is a savory code for Postmates, but then see it's actually EATUP2—the mind raunches then ruches, hiding the swell inspired by that type of thought.

When the rain sounds like the noise machine instead of the other way around.

How many times the re-gifted silk robe must catch a doorknob or stair railing for you to get the hang of slowness.

Set yourself down, flesh vase—until the alarm sends you again to your hustle.

The little mouse of your muscle scurrying as you admire your rotating tricep.

No longer shying away from indulgence—the brazenness of pleasure, the raisin of pleasure, rehydrating.

The end of the alphabet, the alphabet's rest.

To walk to delete a mood rather than add to it.

Never turned the house fan to auto—"the cool air about them" summing up the fan's biography.

Erratic rain, rat-ta-tat-tatting—you check the weather again as if the sky's supposed to be texting you or the rain is the sky's text—a sequence of emojis on the asphalt.

Dug a French ditch, imported from the thinking of Henry French rather than the country.

Binary hair.

An aerial view shows us the city is mostly scalp, parted here, parted there.

Hard to gauge other people's levels of comfort—more single-floor than high-rise.

We wondered what asterisks on the shirts of some figures in the mural signi-fied—death perhaps or a snowflake pattern meant to suggest a season or to create coherence among a motley crew—the first regulars?

Like girls on phones in the back rows of movie theaters, the more innocuous attention seeking.

One suspects a refusal to record because of what the record might show.

Dear ocean, I know you can't come to me.

A Ziploc bag of sand that causes questions at security.

You still don't buy the bar's justification for selling a drink called Strange Fruit in honor of Black History Month, yet we do drink to dead men, raise a glass, coddle our ice as if it were infant water, maybe given a chance at a fluid existence, if long enough let be.

Entanglements.

You wouldn't have the paper fox head if he weren't so good with patience and glue—for the love of zeugma, for the love of zoo-moms, giraffe mom, elephant mom, eel mom, mother of sickness—the mom even he exhibits, your own mom ever fatherless, furthering from you.

What wrong does this take place inside.

Moved by a story of a riding crop that becomes a guarded cypress.

A dedication on a two-seater tree swing one must move uphill toward, a required optimism.

The search yields few results—something about our terms.

Among those for whom debt is easier to accumulate than wealth.

*

You are a tie on the neck of the mountain—stay sitting with your back exposed.

Numbingly, the toothache plant does what its name tells it to do.

Everyone looks good with the backdrop of a soft brick wall.

Enthusiasm around the comment "we could sushi"—a glimmer of litigiousness.

Had to look up squall.

The sound of nails being sorted.

Funnel cake truck with handwritten signs—a churro-shaped "1" but no churros otherwise on the menu.

Lilac not lacking.

Pause to argue death from above or death from below.

A refusal to forgive.

She breaks the only human.

Happy, but—but happy (chiasmus, a hug inside language, a pocket for holding).

I used to trust words more.

You were already beautiful.

*

A last last day.

Wood fed to the insatiable backseat of a car.

We set off sensors.

Sometimes all one needs to do is ask for an umbrella and an umbrella appears.

Hold my water, and I'll call you my aqueduct.

At sea, on land, and online.

The stranger holding up to the window his 3-stack of pancakes with strawberries and cream, for which you erect your enthusiasm.

Thumb up like overlooked hardware on the otherwise smooth surface of the table.

Gathering the Nick & Nora glasses that you had assumed wrongly must be hand-washed.

To disorient yourself with a daydream of matsutake mushrooms—unclear if you've had one before knowing what it was, a mushroom worth pining for— edible haiku, though isn't a tenet of all haiku digestibility?

Your tears bring my own soluble eyes out of my face—my own water-ant, tunneling out the farm of my sand-colored cheek.

The impressive cellular makeup of white oak.

A fence a yard resists.

People you've never met have spare keys with no clue where they fit.

*

You want too much matcha for the mouth-feel—the sound.

The meeting runs over like an unattended cup at the refrigerator water dispenser that one has to move the fridge to clean up, which is to say: it's tedious.

The awkwardness of two people carrying a floppy mattress, a size too big for a room.

Each country has its narratives and needs its tellers and its banks and its waterfront parking.

Carbonation: a sizzle that stays in your throat—a sizzle that says so in your throat.

What indeed.

I wouldn't call that gait walking so much as pacing.

It's not that you're avoiding goodbye, it's just that you don't want to build that door inside yourself, not either that frame.

To simply repeat your sadness: *I'm sad, I'm sad*—hitching yourself like a triumphant set of oxen to your own sadness, to pull yourself through.

For a while you wonder if you were the one to put goji berries in the little white bowl and fail to eat them.

A walk to the kitchen counts.

One must drink *before* thirst—what else must come before and to whom must we bring ourselves (you'll say no one, simple as a wind picking up a leaf—the impact of detachment).

An hour isn't always long.

Inevitable as a bird leaving.

*

Counting laps: breaststroke, breaststroke, freestyle, free, breaststroke, breast, backstroke, back, breaststroke—that delicious pool, *stst*, healing the break in *brea-roke.*

Hospitality and poetry: two types of attention I love, yes, love.

Like a food item being what's special today.

A comic drawing of a finger sandwich waving with a finger-less hand from a tea tower.

It is said one dives into research.

Thinking of interpretation: what you thought was meant by "land-shark" when you first read it in a text—not as sexy as what your friends, girlfriends, performed, while you hummed the two-note motif of *Jaws*, laughing at their fins.

Joy can lead you places other than satisfaction.

A description of shark finning: removing fins from sharks and discarding the rest of their bodies back into the ocean.

Unable to swim, one sinks.

Let loose that thought—a dog some unpeopled field might rescue, away from roads.

The thought is phlegm, caught in the throat-way of obsession.

Cheer yourself with this serum said to promote cellular turnover—welcome a new generation of cells.

What life will you get with them—what life will you give.

A hangnail hardening on your hand.

*

Family doesn't so much seem ties that bind as it does barnacles you're scraped on when pulled under the hull of a boat.

I kid but am not with child.

Spent a few days reading an ode to regret and floating in that shame—damp hammock, dirty tank.

That that "period of one's life" is drawn out rather than final—a point in time we line up behind.

A dehumidifier will not solve this.

Our flesh isn't a thing we get to keep, no matter how we care for it.

Sell that information to someone else.

A flapping sound.

The day you no longer had access to your bar of space.

Same job as always—but what's the job of always?

He's pinched his callous into a teeny wall I balance my finger atop—repulsed and drawn (the abjection of tenderness)—toenails he clipped from the toes of my feet in an ice-cream-coated ramekin on the couch.

Have used myself as food.

A list of reasons a house may be tented—you can laugh even if you don't believe the house got tired of sleeping outside.

We wait to be told to reenter.

*

Each day starts with a search for more space for memory—dying laptop, dying earth.

Sadness a pen you can't get out of—a pen you can't get ink out of either, regardless of your wrist's best flick.

You take "love you forever [broken heart emoji]" to mean another death.

A small glass parrot positioned so as to be whispering to a small glass cardinal, supervised by a larger-but-still-small ceramic turtle.

The next cat should be named Derrida's, apostrophe like a second tail.

Ask what you need to ask.

A syllabus of donkeys, by any of their names—syllabass, syllaburro.

Championing the Swiss chard on the podium of your molars or canines—a little hard to tell with just your tongue.

The tiger lilies dripping their tiger blood, their own poachers, but avoiding a vase-fate (flower cage)—give me my melodrama, give me my tears.

A blocked duct swelling an eyelid.

You count in your mind docks and piers where you walked to the end and the times

you turned back.

Baby sharks illegally kept.

Too often thinking it will be easy to stop somewhere for water along the way.

Fewer offers than one had hoped.

*

Imagining a pedicure for a foot a snow.

Wet flip-flops on pavement.

A jasmine-huffing party underway, under nose.

The sky looks like it's using.

Having read Hemingway's description of trees right before moving through the Smokies—that he shortened himself into a verb (Hem)—to mend, to alter.

Tutored by resorts, we call our marriage "Adults Only" rather than childless.

All the lanes taken.

A store doesn't really have a sister, but a second location—good enough stock.

Fewer cicadas today clinging to the pool safety rope lines—one making a raft out of the dead Hercules beetle, divine hero, again.

No cash on you, so no cone.

Wish to call the minor god from now on a godlet, like an owlet, but not so young or even small.

You learn it's the slugs eating your leaves—"your" leaves; you learn anthos
is a flower and anthology, a bouquet.

He blames the sloshing on the glass.

Of course, corruptible: the "o" an engagement ring, slipped onto
whatever stuns.

*

Something off inside myself.

On the dock, an exposed screw and a counting back in one's head to a last tetanus booster—duct tape won't do.

Among the beneficial species, the milk snake whom you have no permission to mourn, having mistaken it for a cottonmouth and having hacked.

The patio *is* covered, in part, but will it *feel* covered in the rain.

Countless meanwhiles and plans at 7:15.

In the trenches of flowers.

Out-of-place place shirts: Miami in Blackwell, St. Croix in Des Moines.

To learn seals are carnivals, like us.

Gore may.

The smallest rabbit making a balance beam of the raised bed's edge.

Good chance of getting the villain edit even being yourself.

That lake-bagging has nothing to do with displacing any lake.

Try apple cider and vinegar with "the mother" and water (another mother), try soda water and bitters, try a chalky tablet.

Careful what you add to your cup.

*

A sensitivity reader and the tenderness of words.

Deep in denial synonyms: rebuttal, non-acceptance, prohibition, nuh-uh.

Not as late as other lates, not as latticed as the light navigating through leafy trees.

His temperature moving between 99.6 and 101.4.

Having frozen minced ginger in an ice cube tray with olive oil.

Having been warned of the bad rectifiers that are out there and the night thieves.

She makes a den of herself, with that bear gazing out of her shirt.

The Milky Way core, when visible, is what you imagine heartburn would look like, if your chest were a Southwestern sky.

The visceral differences in walking away from and walking toward—not about the tide's coyness or the moon's tease—or the sky's dark denim with a sewn-on moon-patch.

A desire to pull one's chest apart like an elevator just barely caught.

When it turns out it's the slugs you love who make holy the leaves.

Screw it, just drink from the pitcher.

A rash behind an ear—a little pebble beach.

Not as late as other lakes.

How flat that belly of cloud.

A dolphin holding a mailbox, a box-holding manatee—what fish is it that carries its own lantern, held out to itself like bright bait?

Water the color of sought-after stones.

I'd likely sit in a hammock of curry.

You gravitate toward an emotional sky.

Promiscuous as the roots of a banyan, your old best form.

Two leaves from a writer's house left in a book's back, apart from its spine.

It's my birthday now every day before my birthday—not about ego, but awe.

A husband washing out then towel-drying a black bralette.

A dream cat, floating.

A dusk must agree to sun's clothes falling to its floor.

Rain riding us as we ride the bikes—good roads that we are.

Water the color of a yawn that emerges in deep restfulness, not boredom.

Seaweed stench—/ grateful to know it: / to make it / to the ocean—again.

*

Watching arcs of tarpon at Pirate's Cove—their own rollercoasters: to engage with water like that, to engage with anything.

Parasailers mimicking jellyfish—they, the lappets and inter-lappets or oral arms, not the bell.

Could have had a ghost thermometer but thought it was an abandoned straw.

You ask the girl likely being sex trafficked the wrong thing in front of the wrong woman.

Someone visiting, allowed to play—the room thick with music, a jelly.

The fish being used to fish for quarters—tourist-bait.

Is it a good friend, helping another friend over a fence she shouldn't be going over.

A mental walk.

Laugh a little typing in "long hard" before adding "seed pod," trying to identify the tree-gift you give yourself from one of Elizabeth Bishop's backyards.

Of course, a mimosa.

To see underwater the sting ray—like a matador hooking wind in his muleta— use its pectoral fins.

To learn one of the persons near us in the ocean is named Mark because, in hearing someone yell to him, we mishear *shark*—you yell out.

Use that filter to make a myth of ourselves.

The way jackfruit unfolds like a miniature book—an autobiology.

*

Her secrete diary, where she keeps a record of all our secretions.

To proclaim *I have no core, I am coreless!* when the child asks if you are cottagecore or gothcore or animecore or indiecore or or or—and seeing now that core's own core is *or*—its own alternative.

Another iguana, green as a virus.

You will take yourself down.

To be as alga is, lacking true stems, lacking true roots.

The kind of child who eats the entire box of Teddy Grahams in one sitting because she doesn't want to separate any of the bears from the other bears.

As soon as you stopped shying away from your mind.

Saw the same day three days.
Mirror death.
To aspire to be a plant because of its lack of desire for sleep.

The heartbeat in the tart was a trick of the heat.

You'll fail but not always.

Can't be legendary without a high C.

We do eat light, just not directly.

*

To identify the cough as "productive"—that it seems to have built something in you (rough composer).

You might as well be a curb, demarcating space, discouraging certain movements.

To thrust the shield of an umbrella, like a pipe cleaner or back of a spoon, carving a smooth path through a smooth material—a pudding or puree; when it comes down, it is the breasts of umbrellas that present themselves to be fed rather than for feeding.

We have the lightening of dragonfly's wings to worry over, too.

Easier now to bring your temper out—little dog, needing to pee.

You watch a car theft you don't realize is a car theft until the owner of the car asks if you saw the theft—big whoops—and meditating on what does it mean to own doesn't address the question of why so many things fail to register.

Texting back and forth about a sighing moon.

Looks like the rain figured out the day's password.

We update "Little Jack Horner," sticking our thumbs in our wine, pulling out gnats instead of plums, applauding our own goodness and extending our applause to the design of the fanny pack, able to secure at its bottom a bottle of red, making itself a red-bottomed fanny, making us laugh—fine to find joy.

As mistaken as each millipede that has wandered in.

Facepalm or palm palm.

Perusing a menu and pondering how would you get that in your mouth.

It's frustrating for all of us, kid, including you, to shut down the pool with your barf—eyes filling up like potholes in a giving weather, the ground a toilet for excess (an excessive toilet).

To live mostly with a broke heart, with a life, mostly turned on—the night holds out a cup the size of a world.